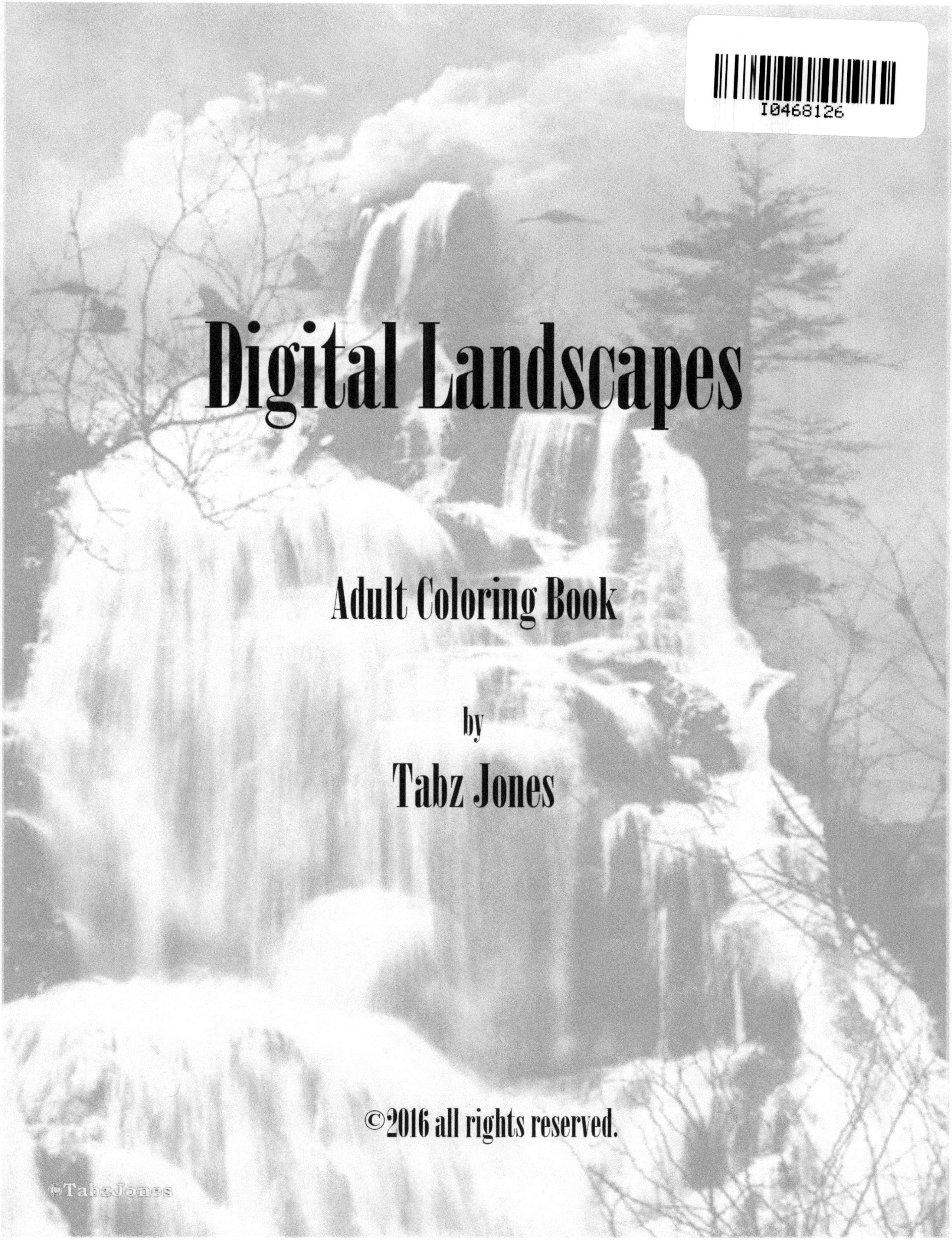

Digital Landscapes

Adult Coloring Book

by

Tabz Jones

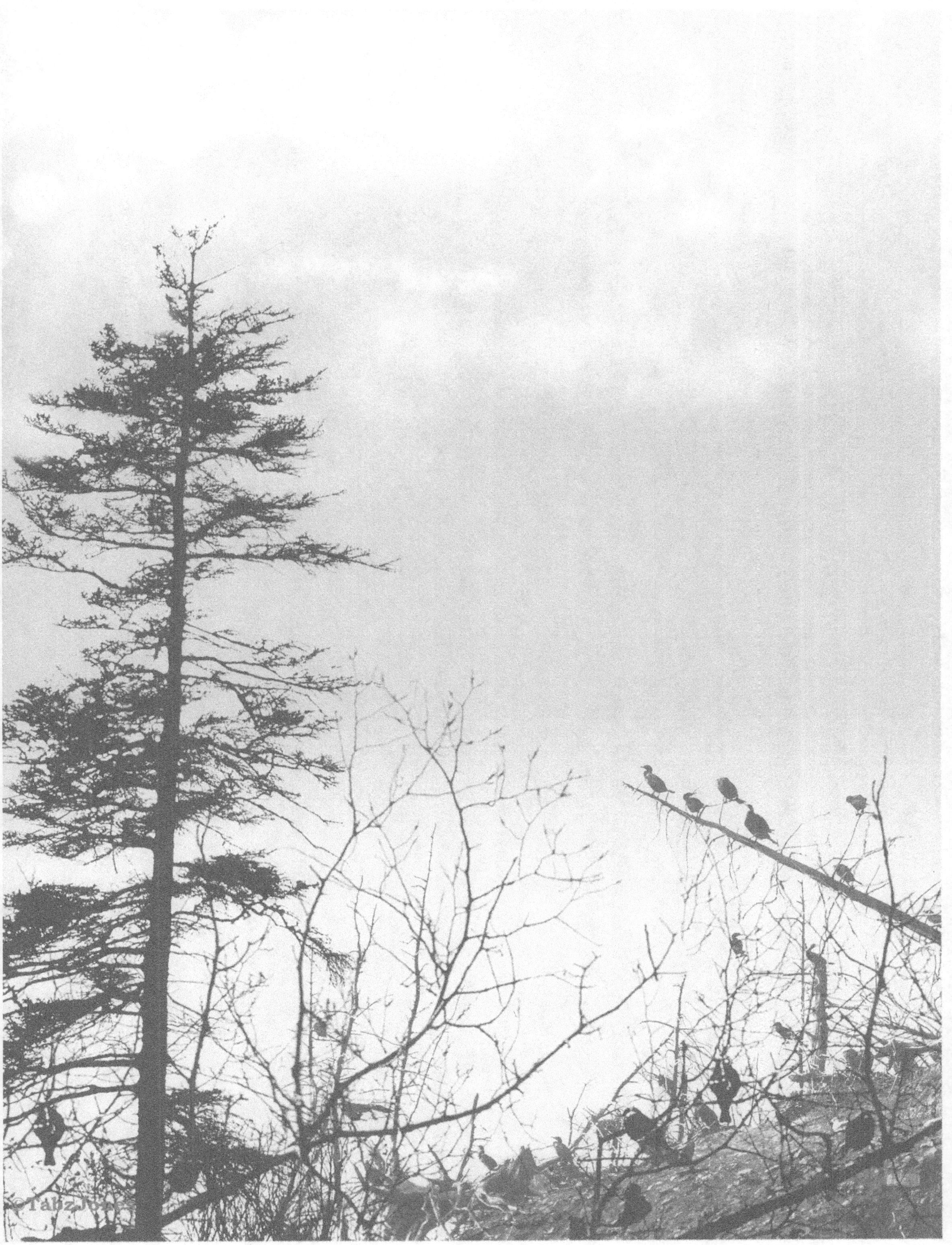

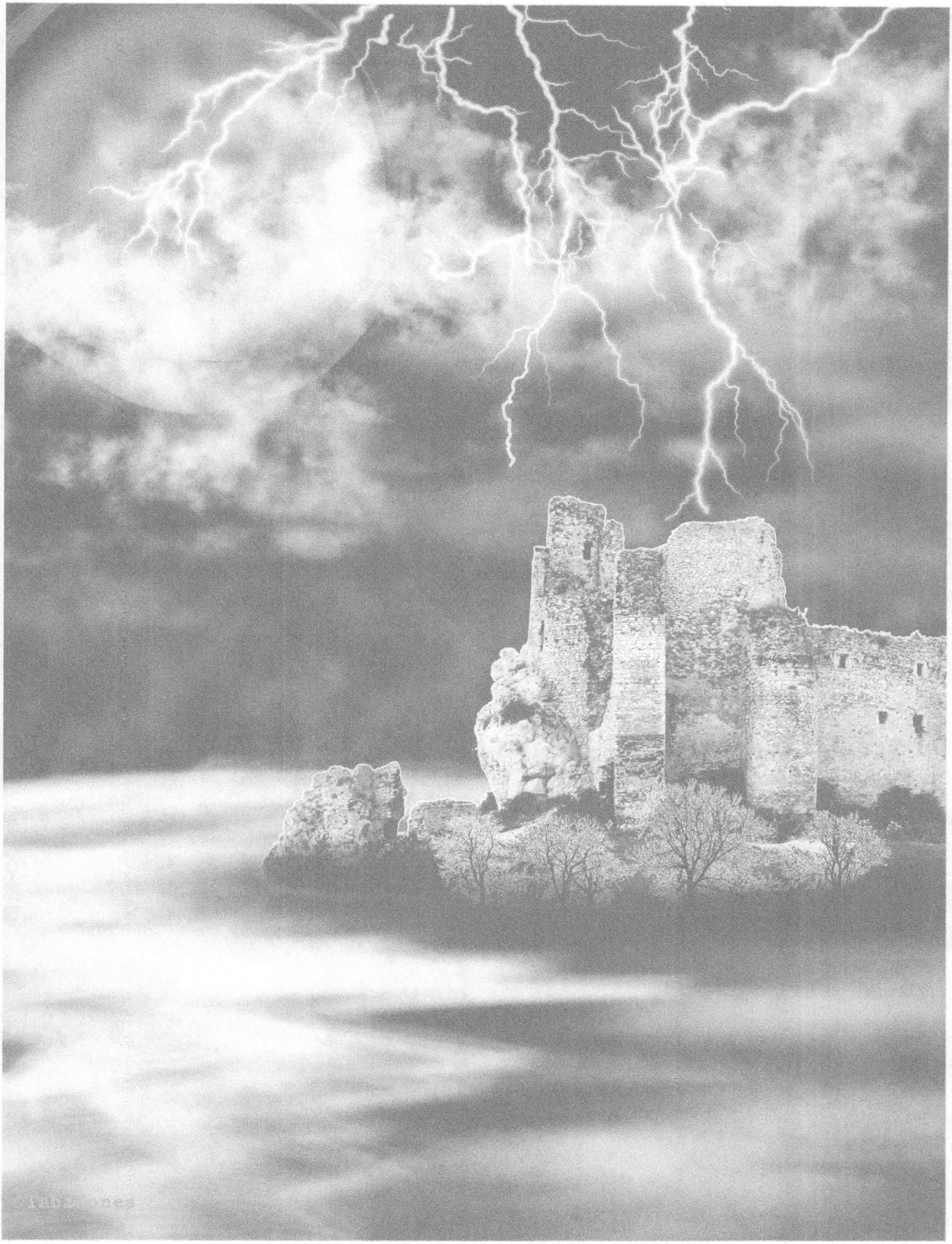

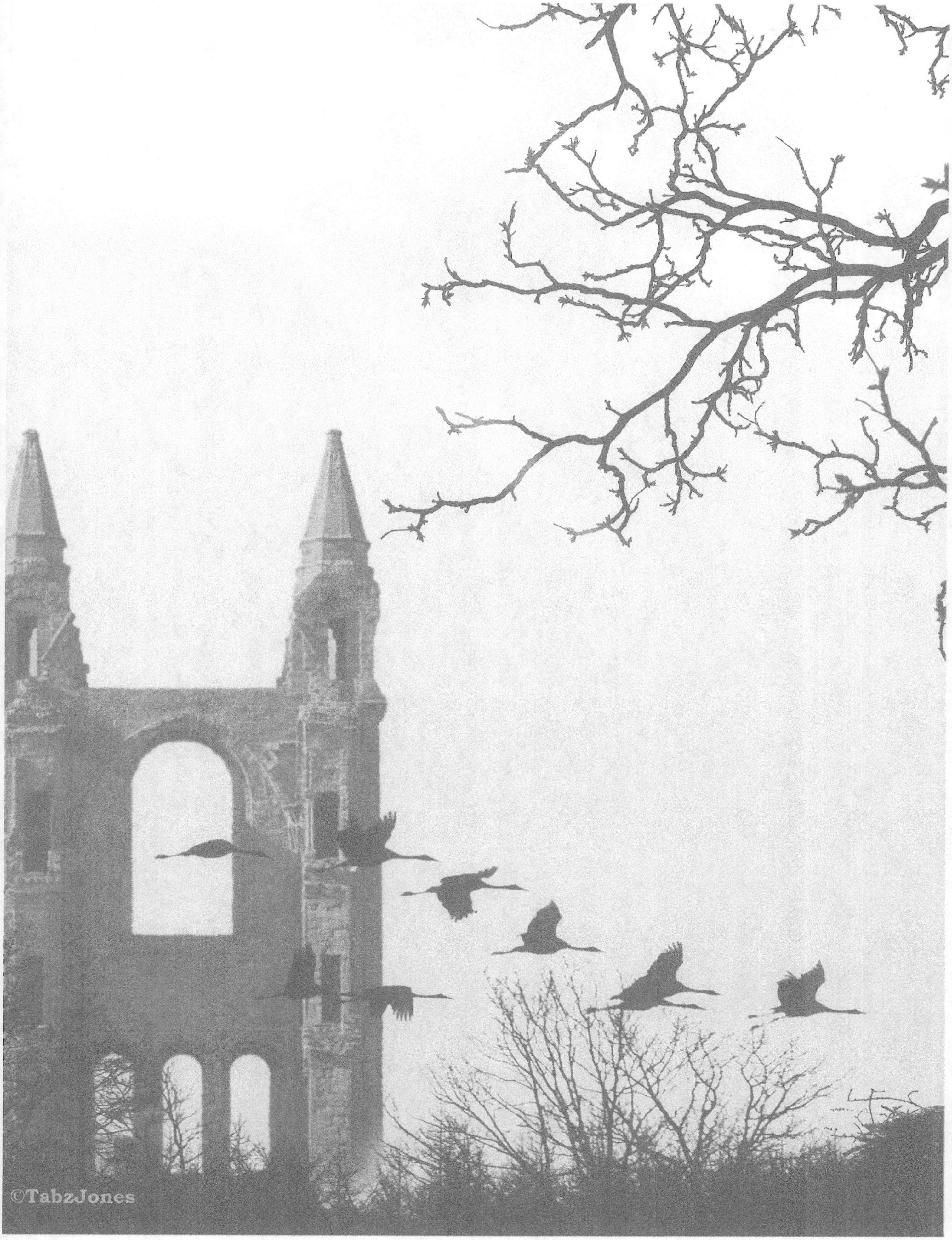
©TabzJones

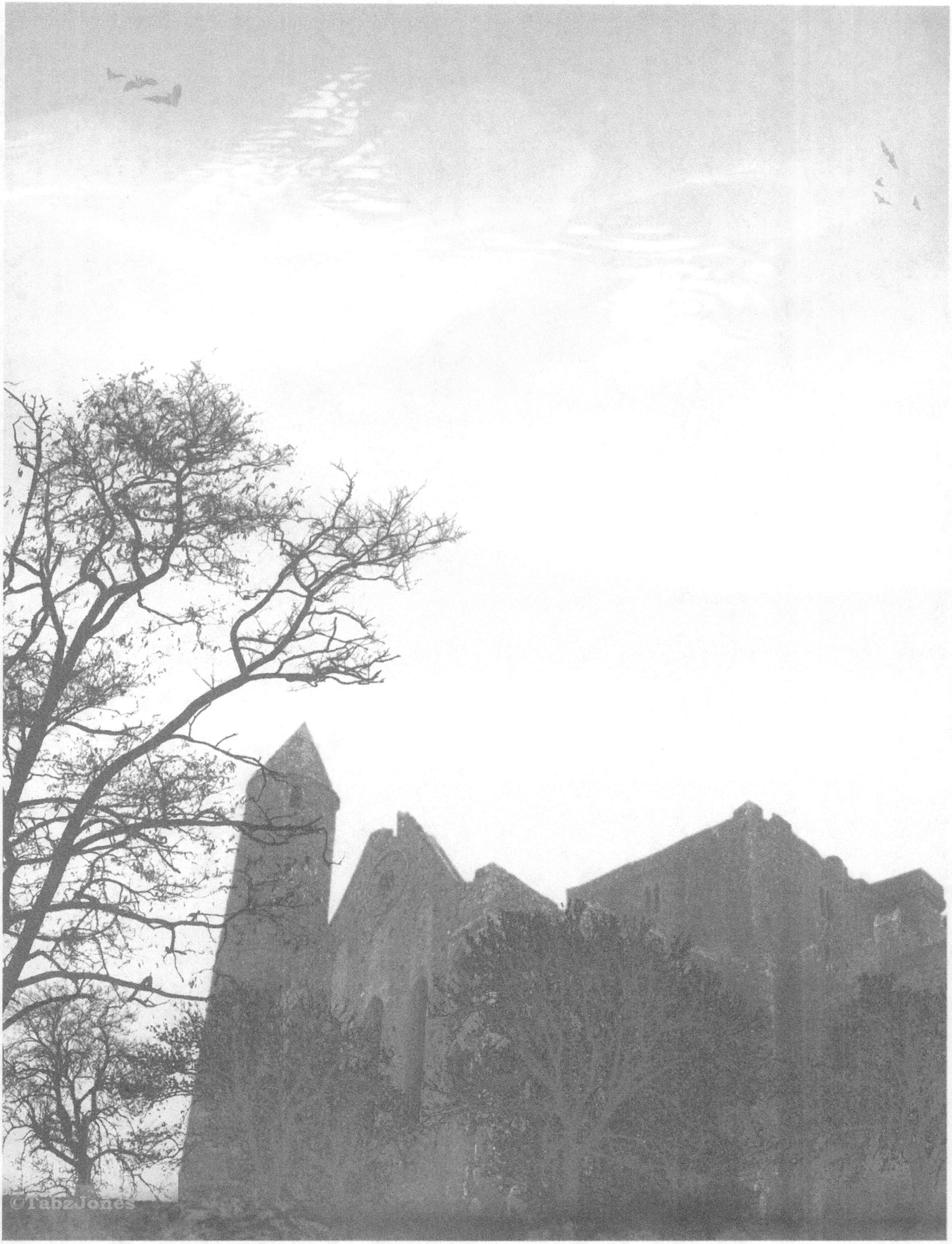
©TabzJones

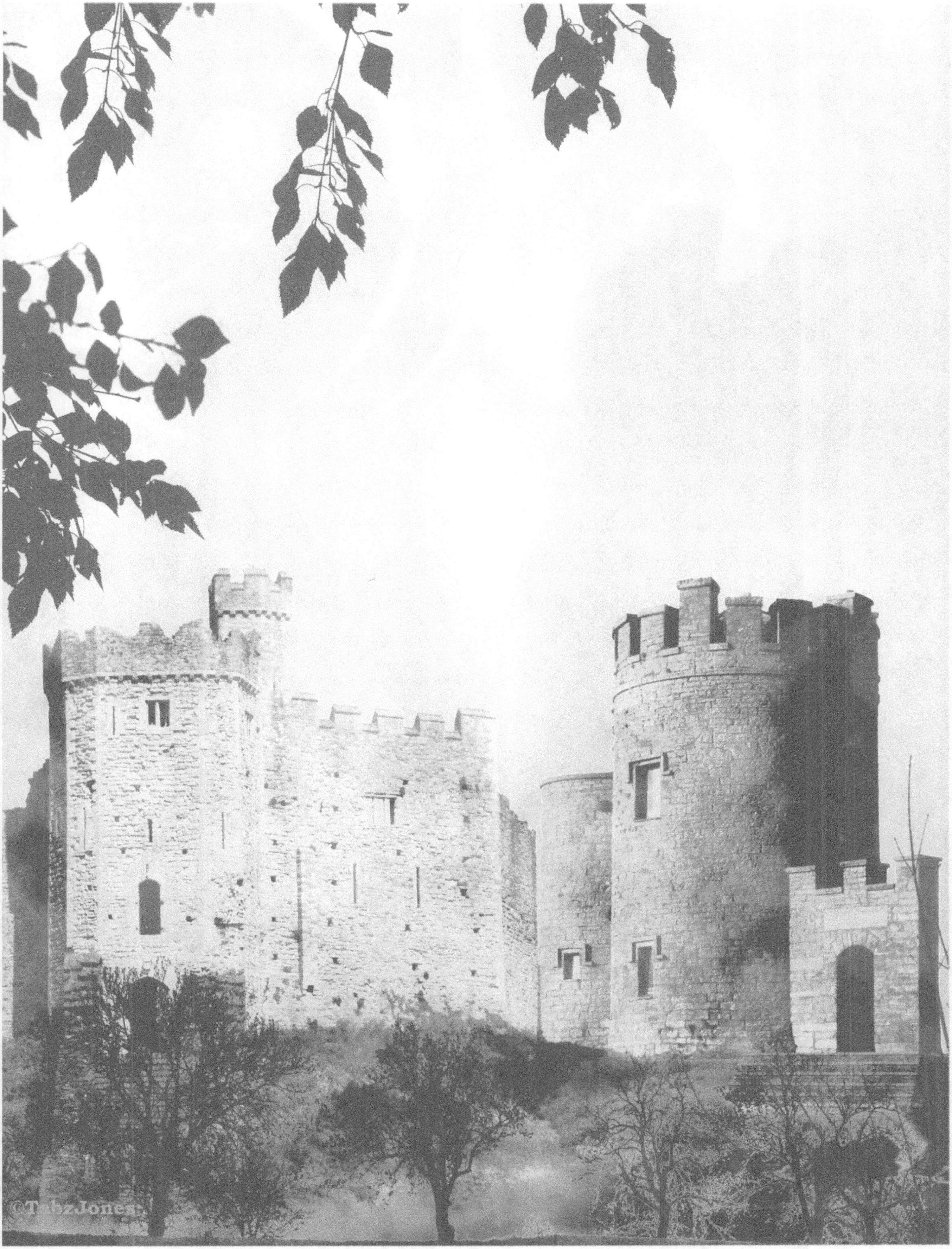
©TabzJones

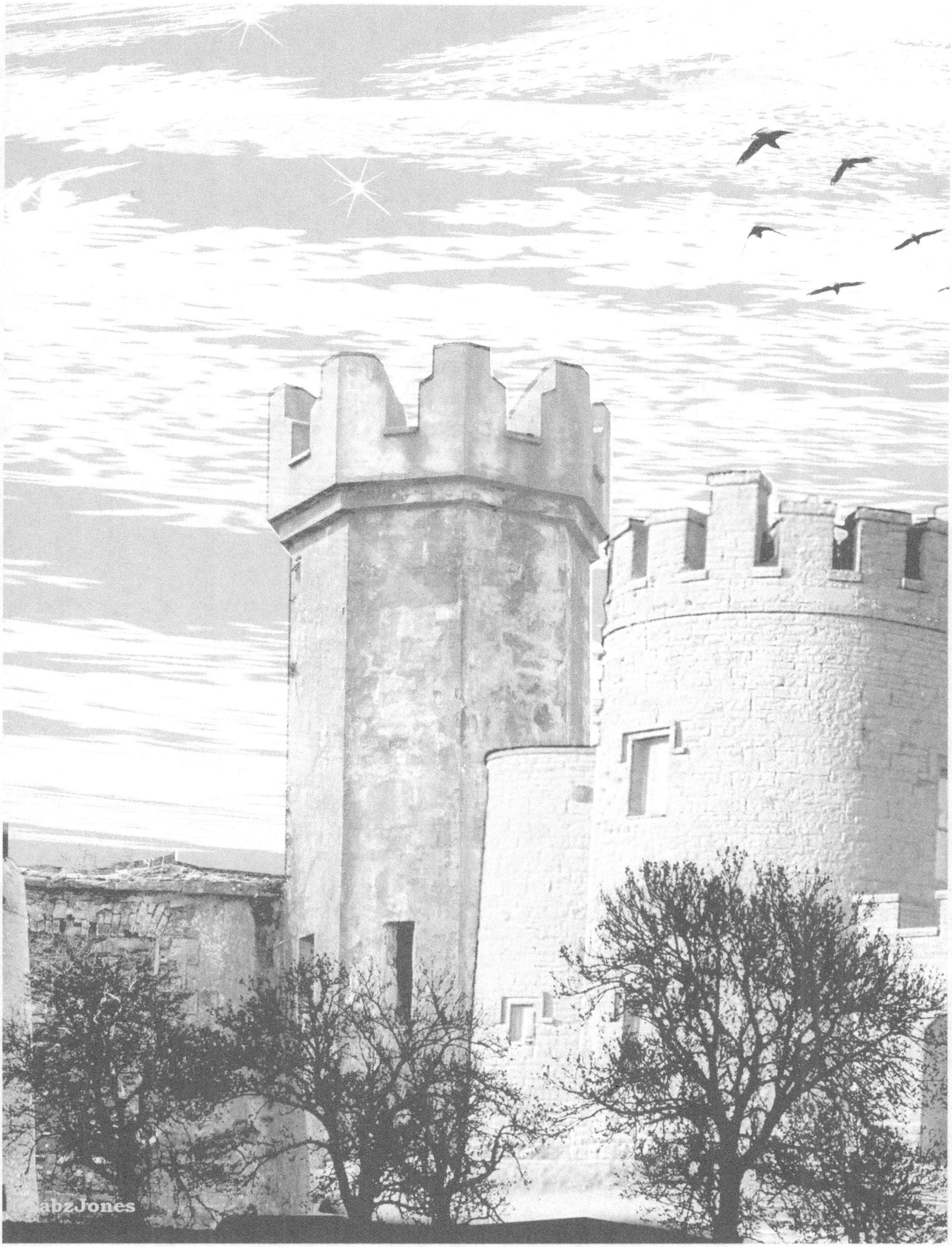
abzJones

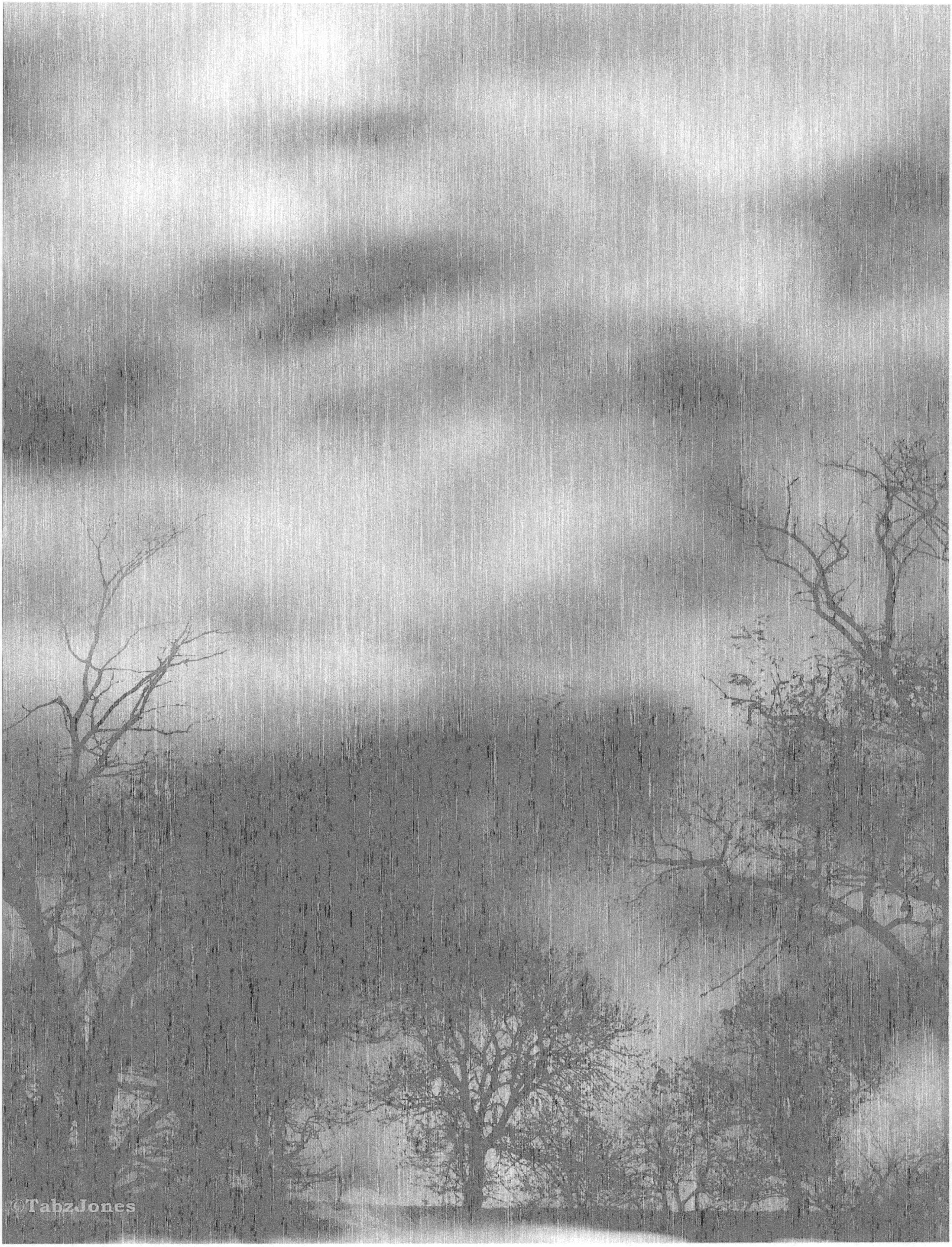
©TabzJones

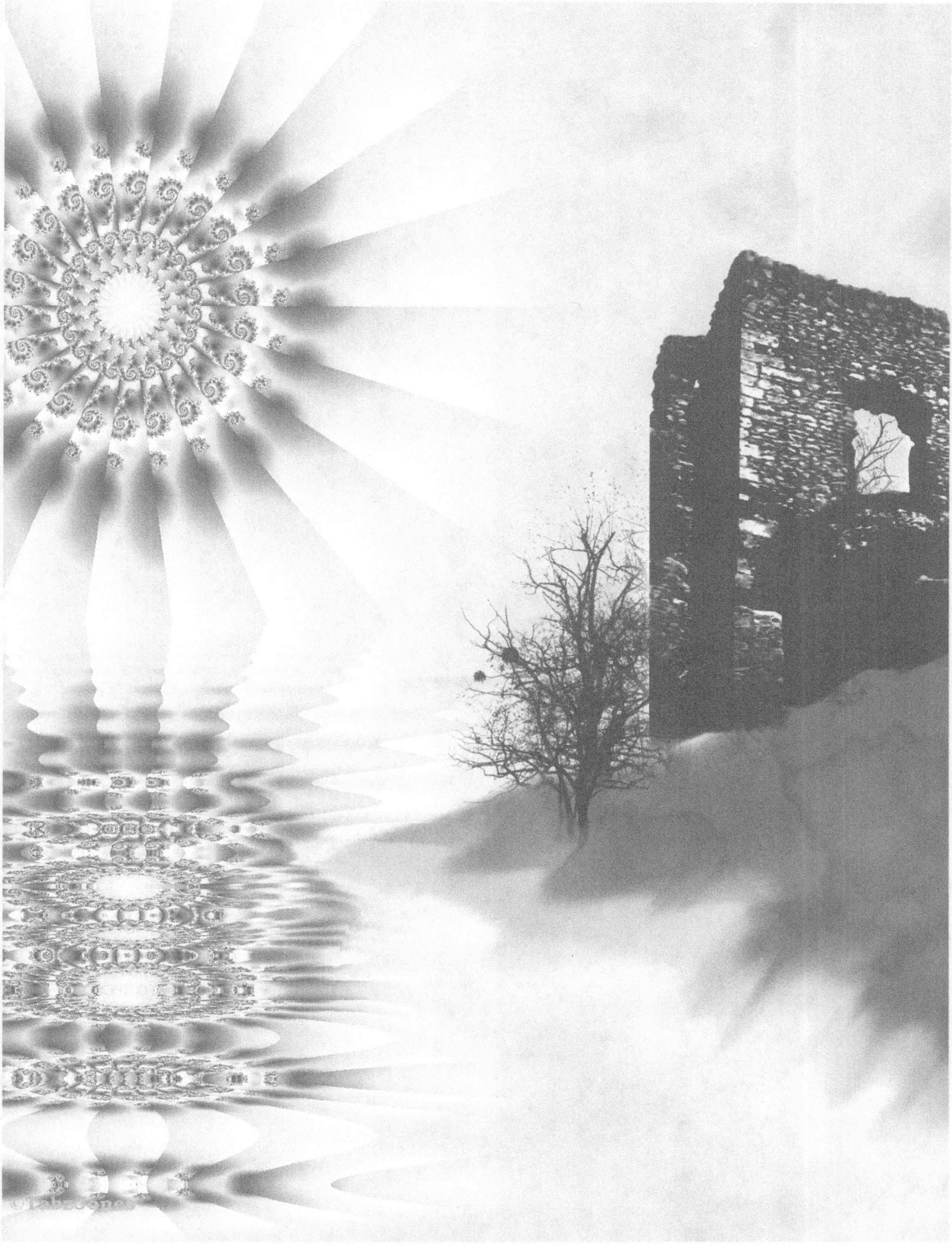

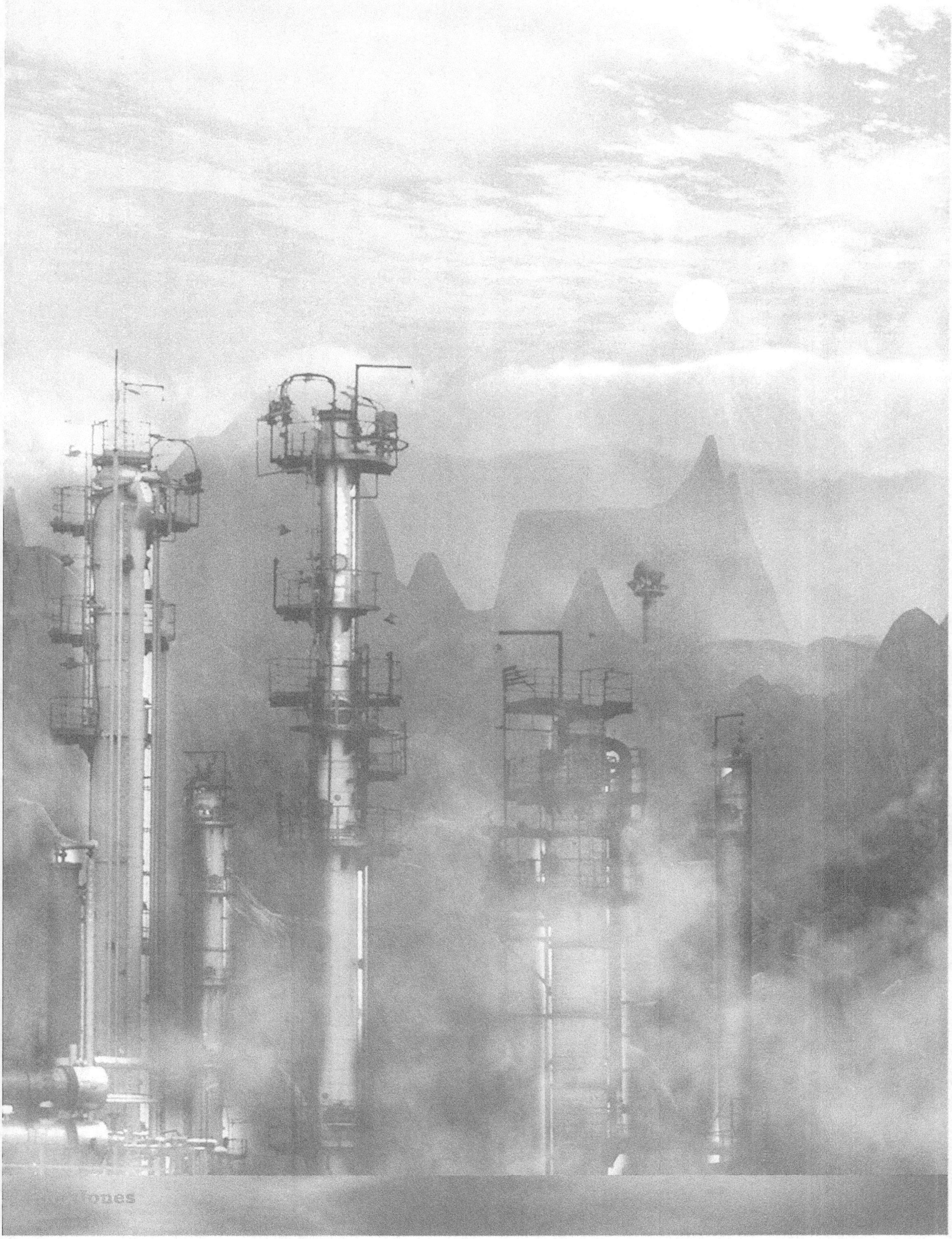

©TabzJon

©TabzJones

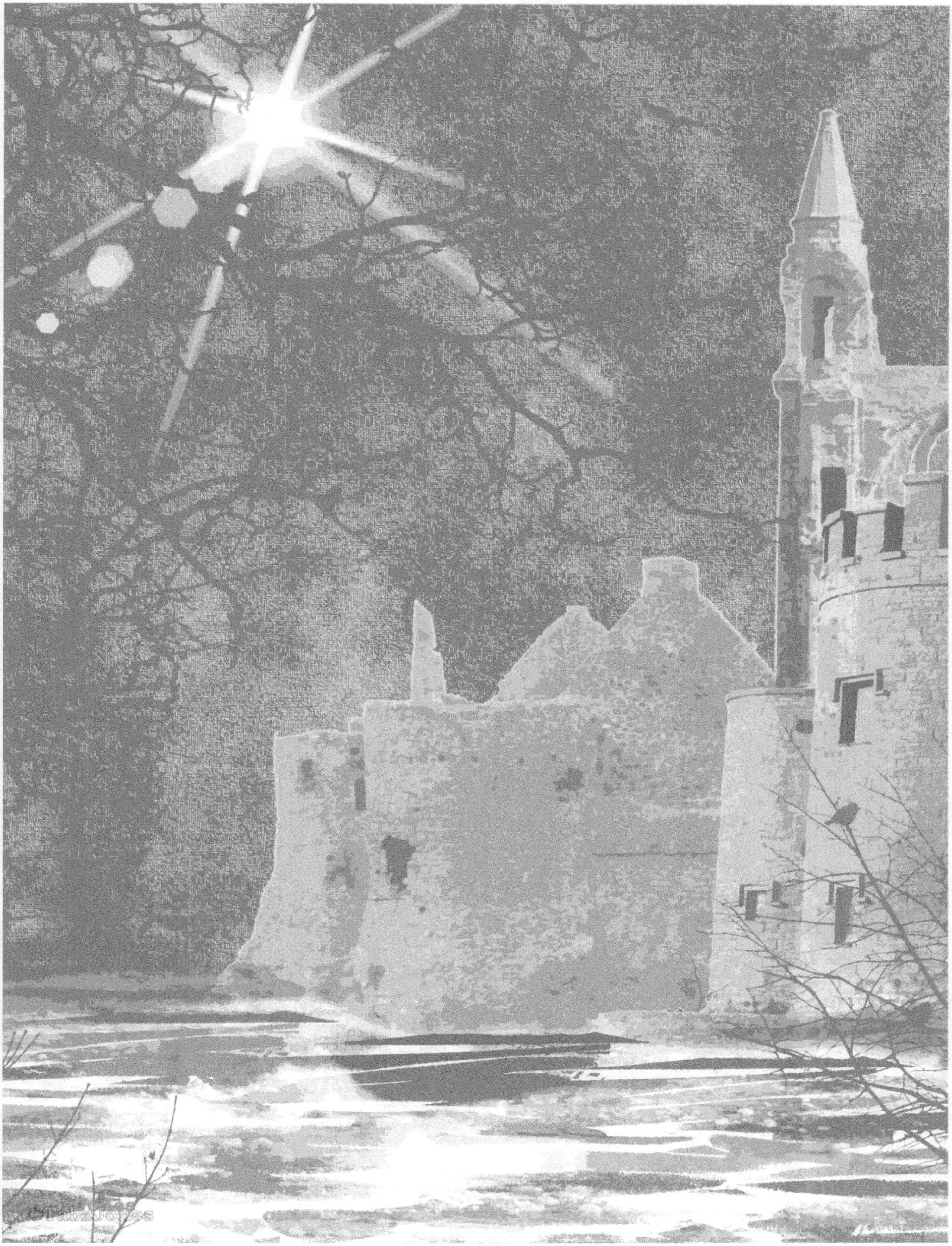
©TabzJones

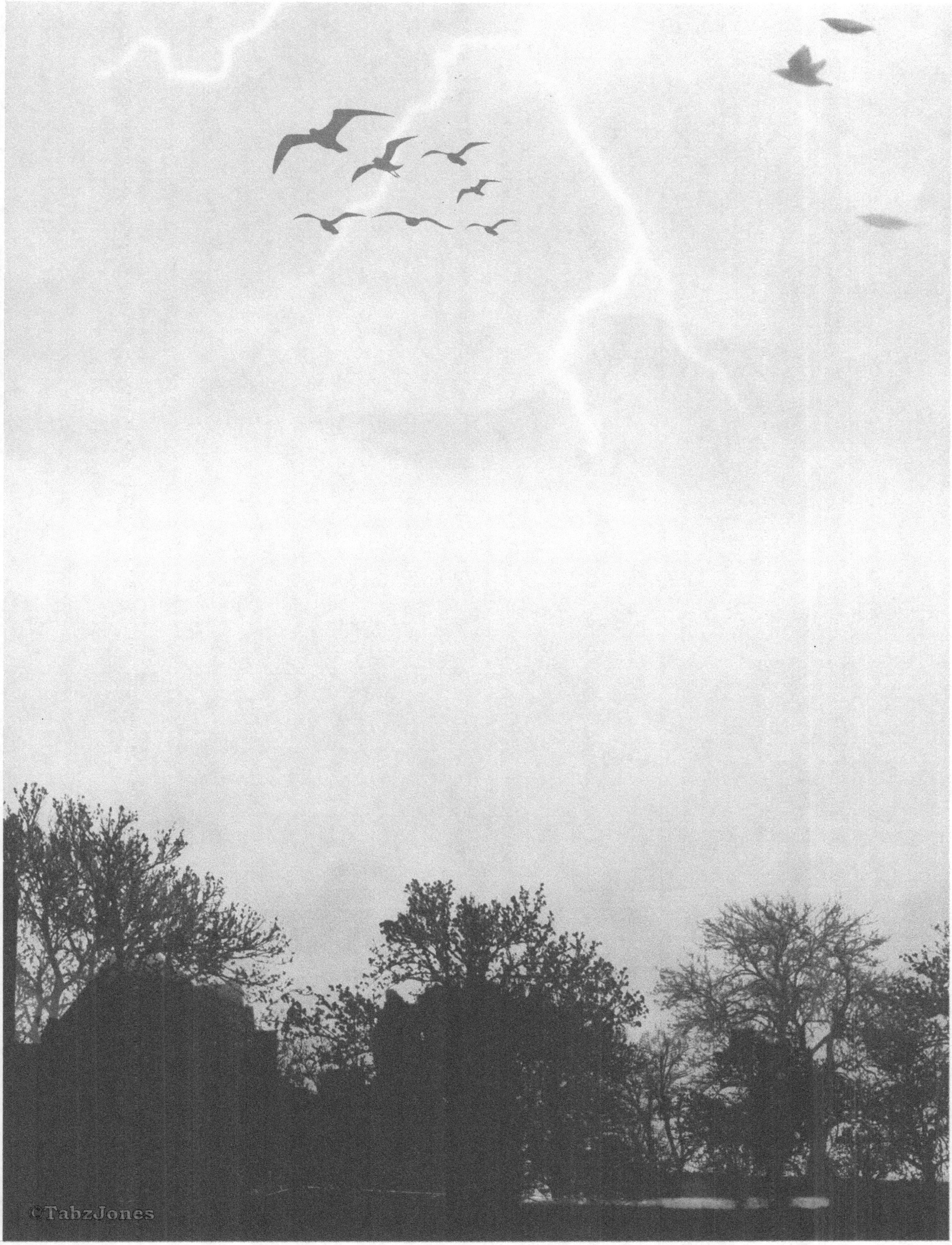
©TabzJones

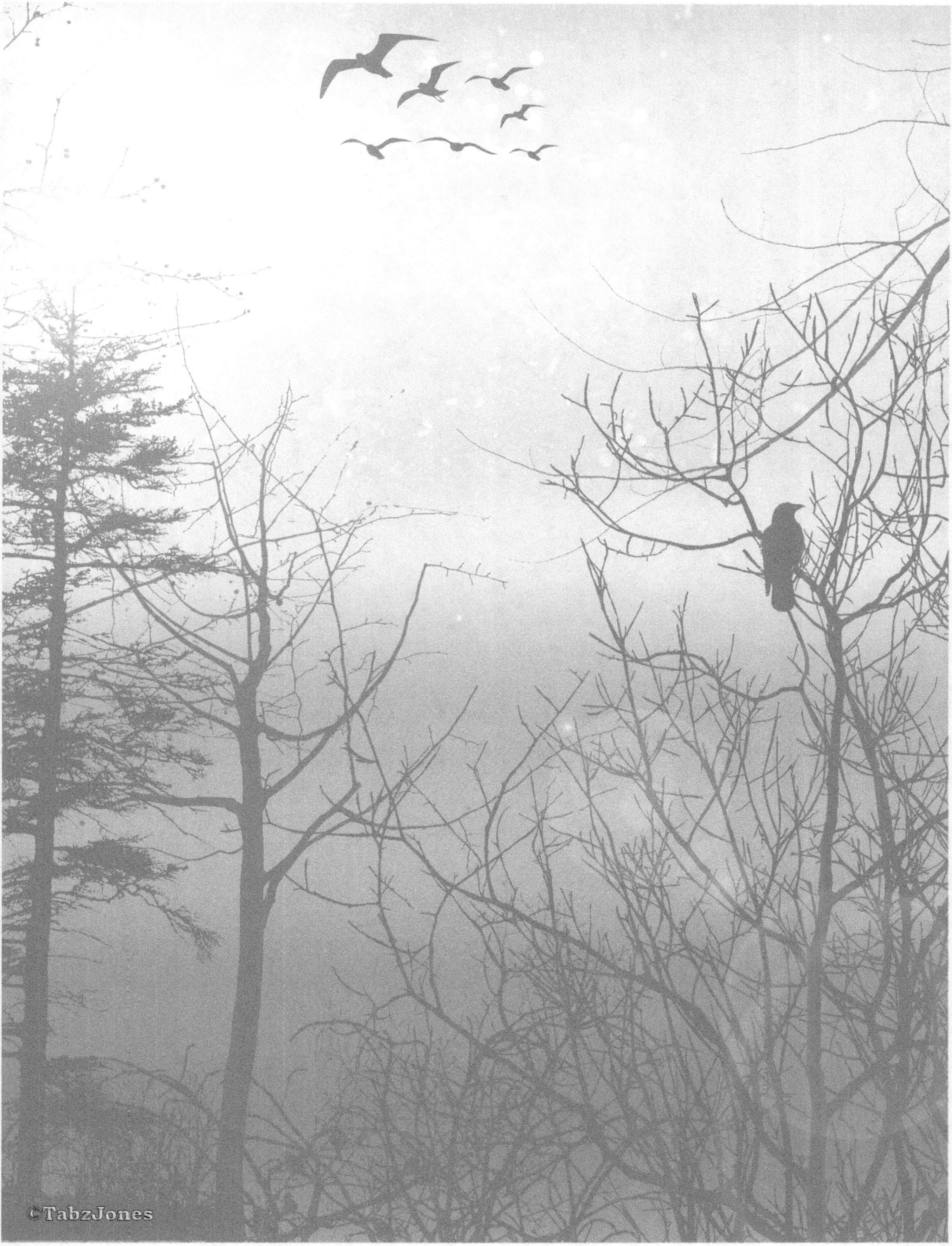
©TabzJones

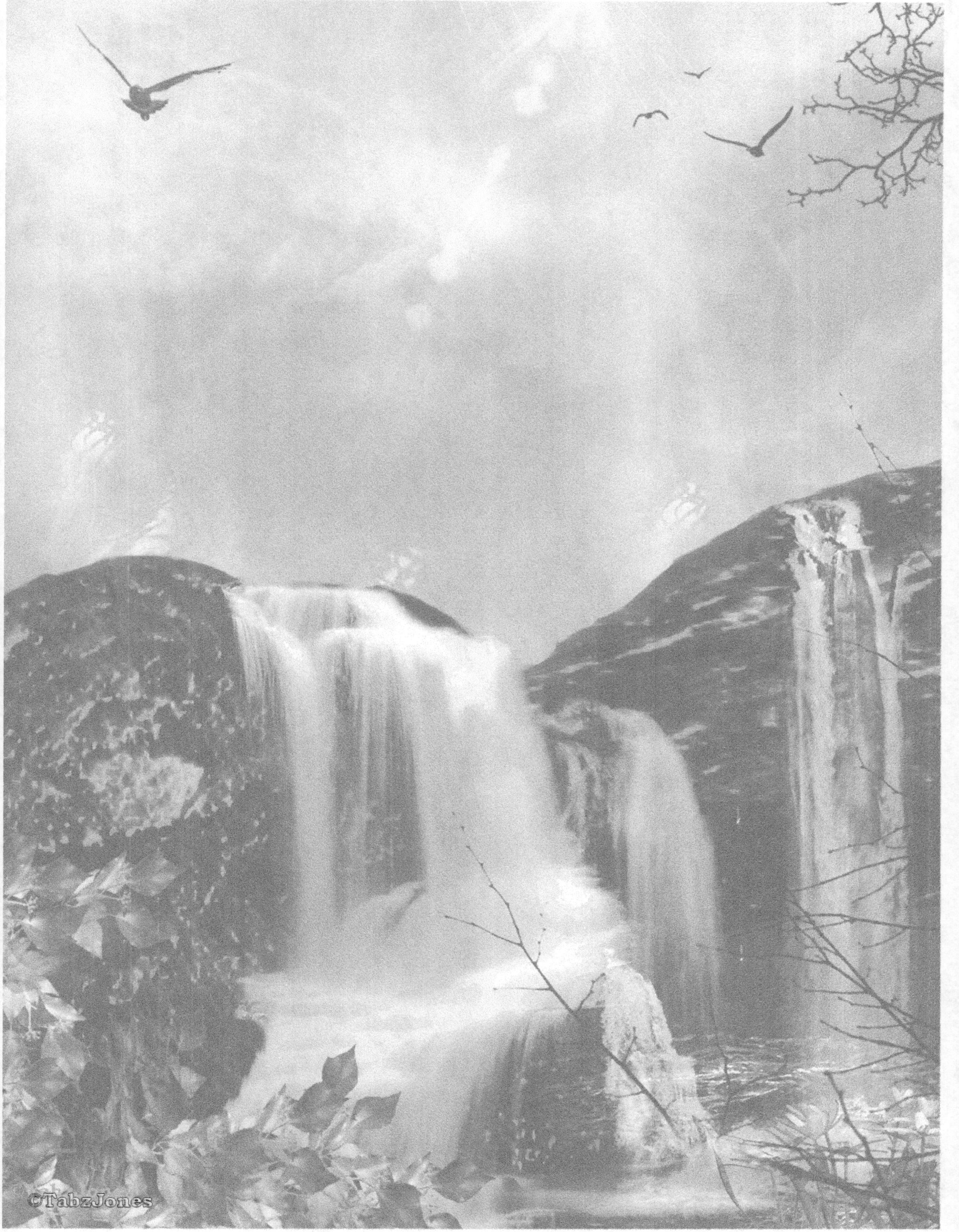
©TabzJones

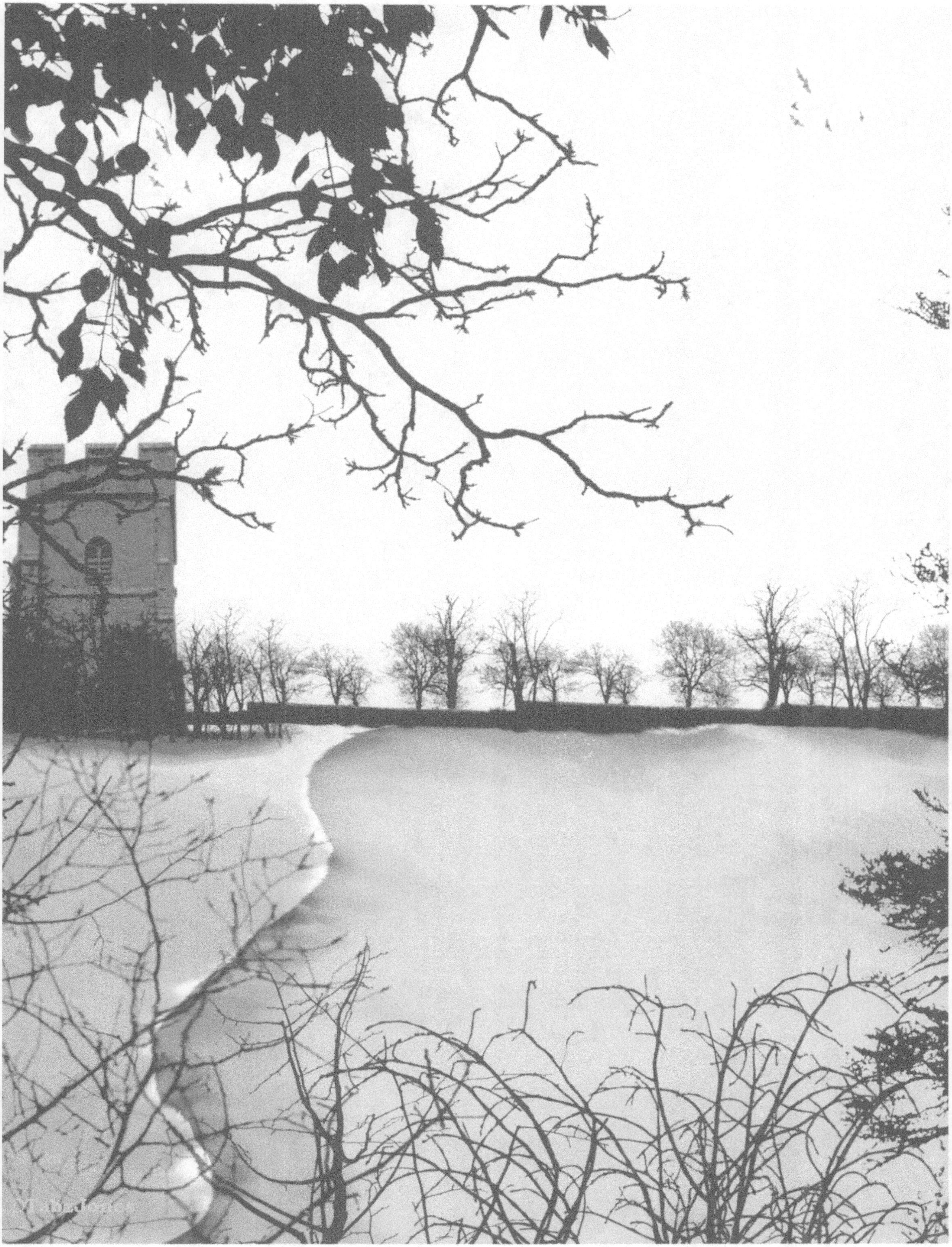

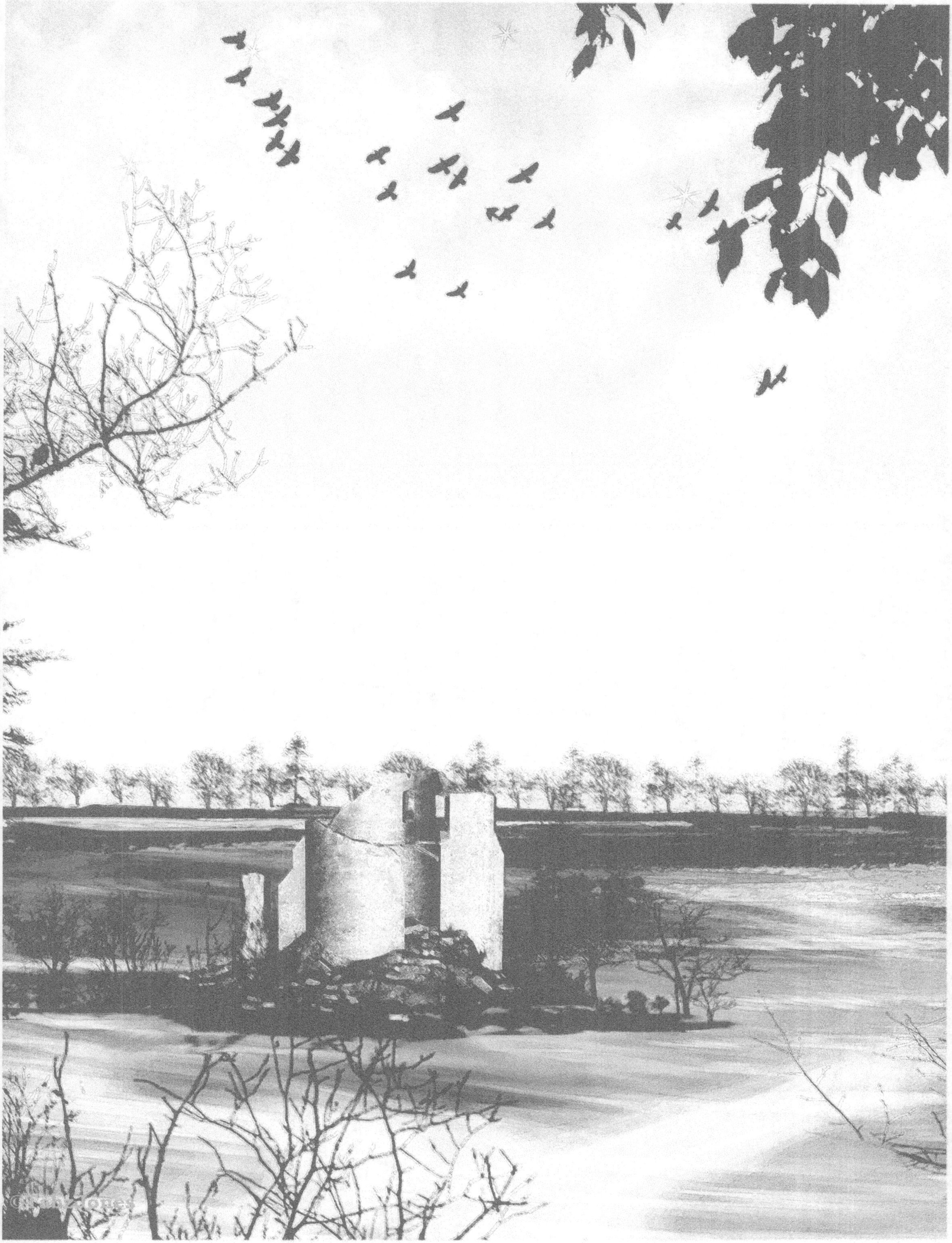

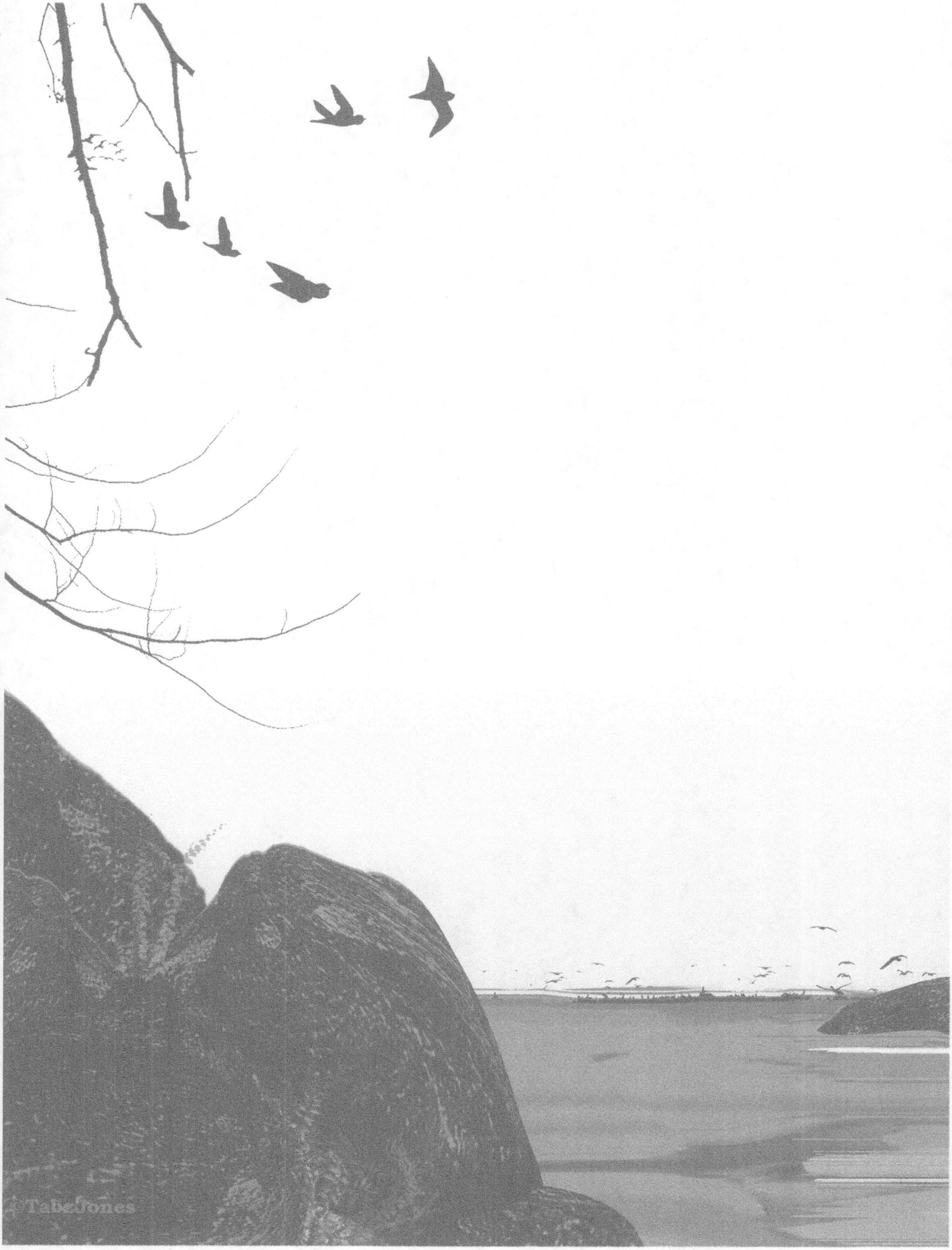
TabeJones

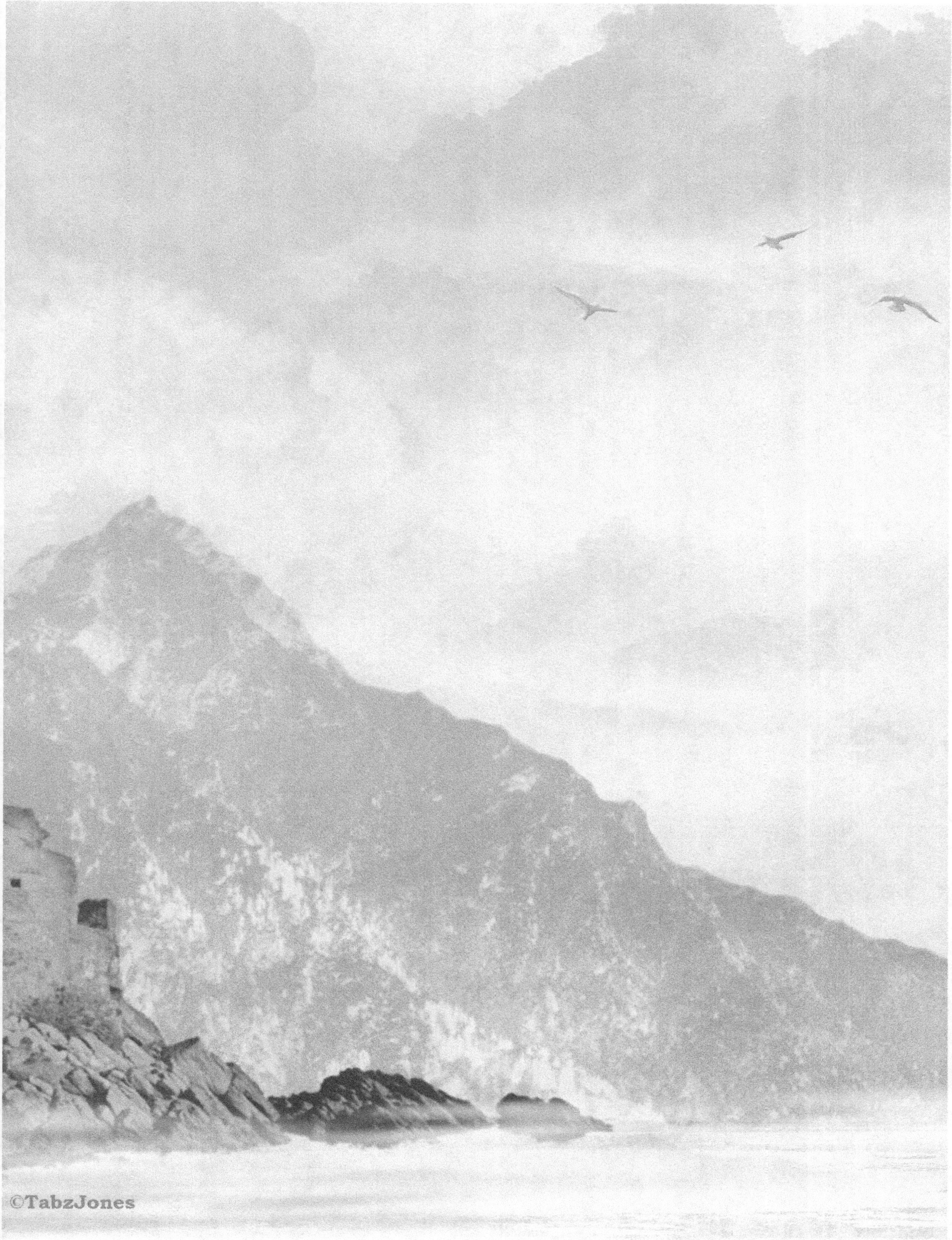
©TabzJones

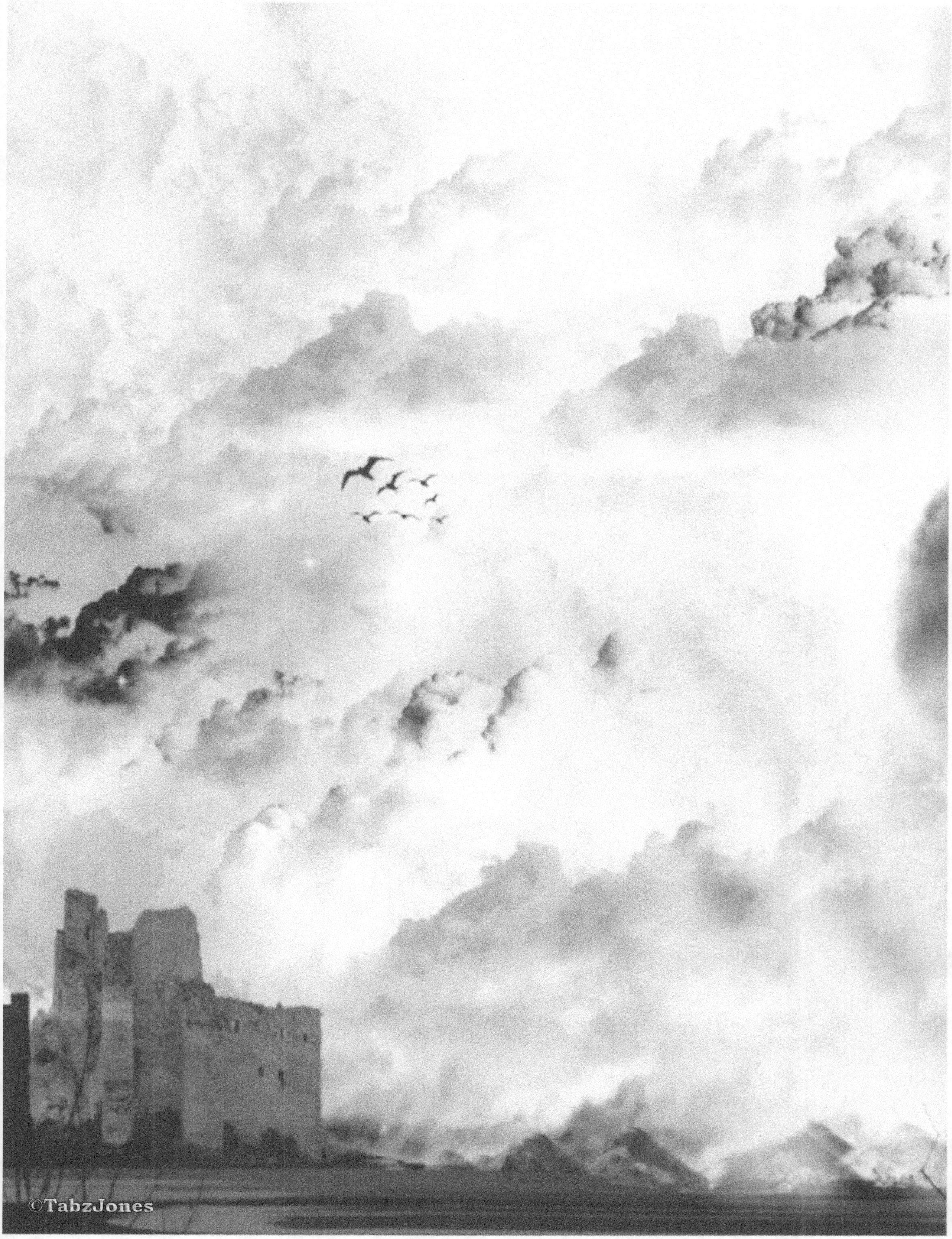
©TabzJones

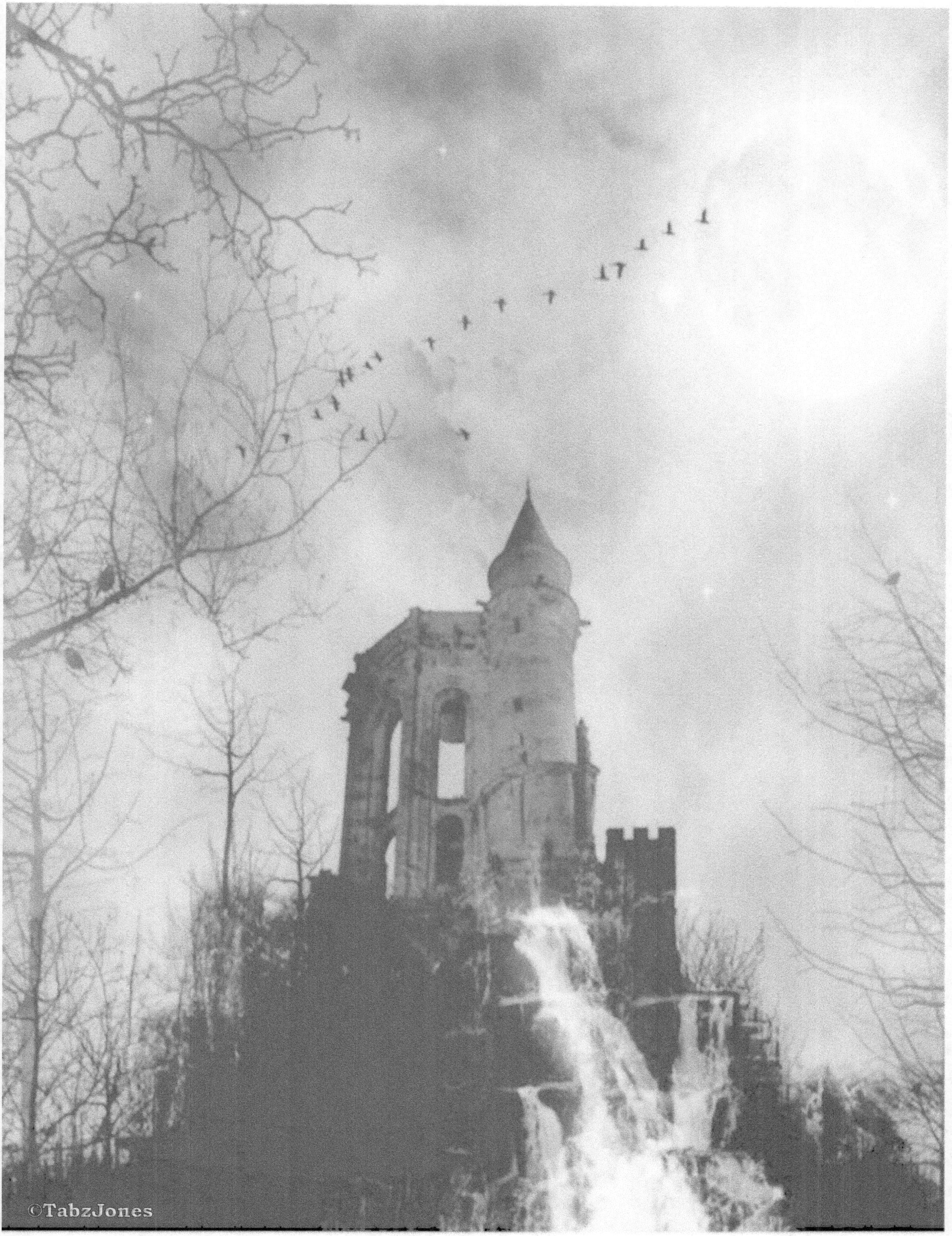
©TabzJones

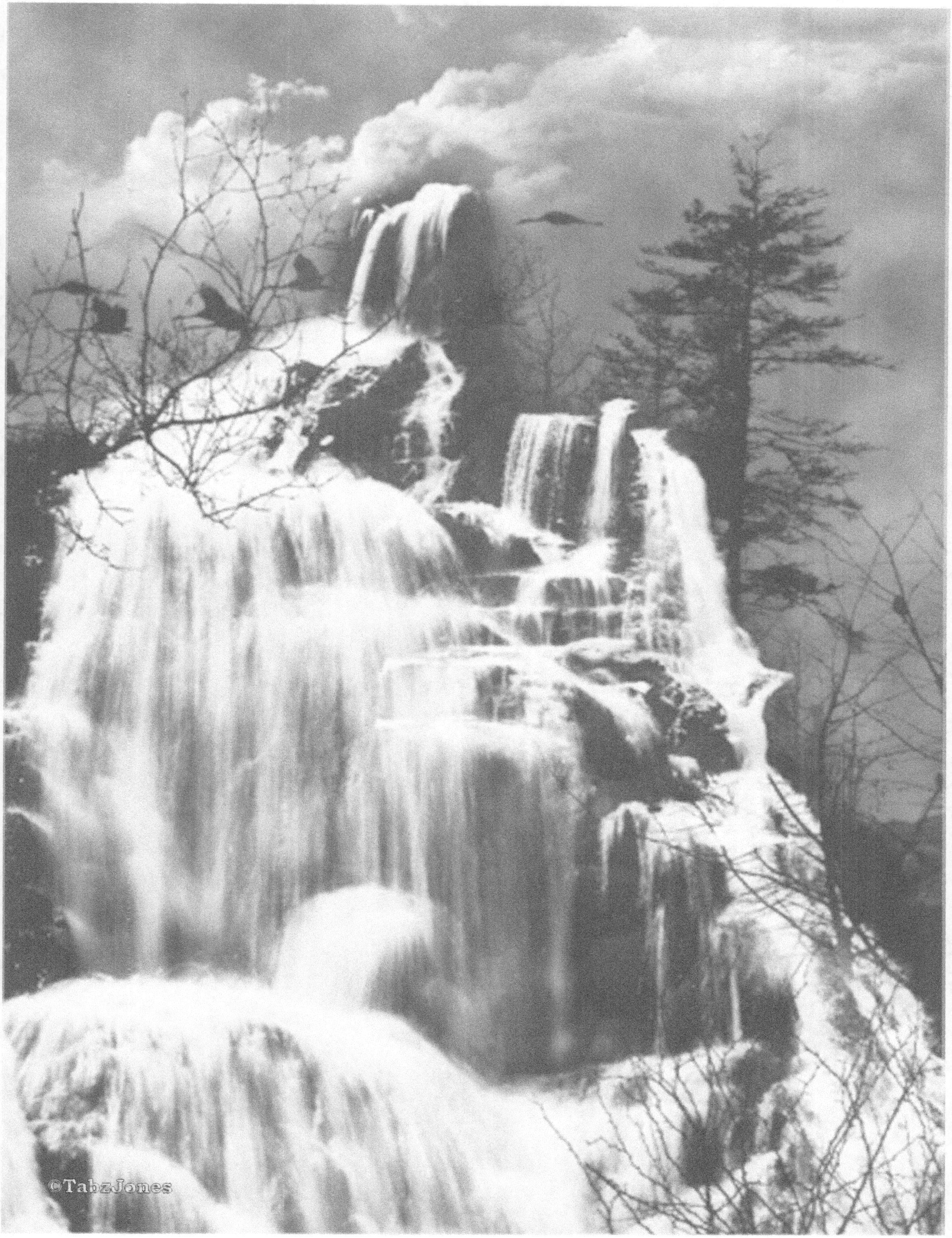
©TabzJones

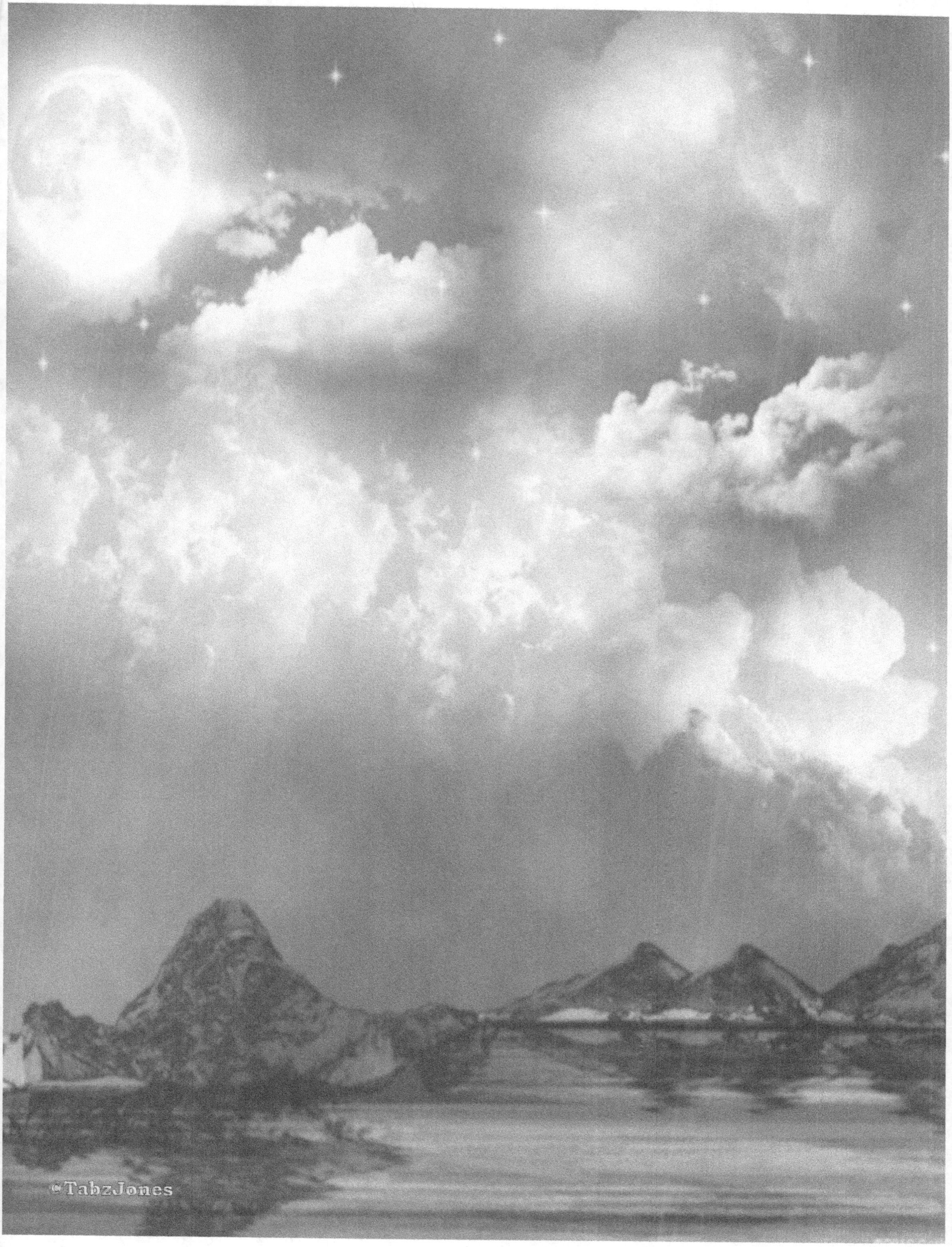
©TabzJones

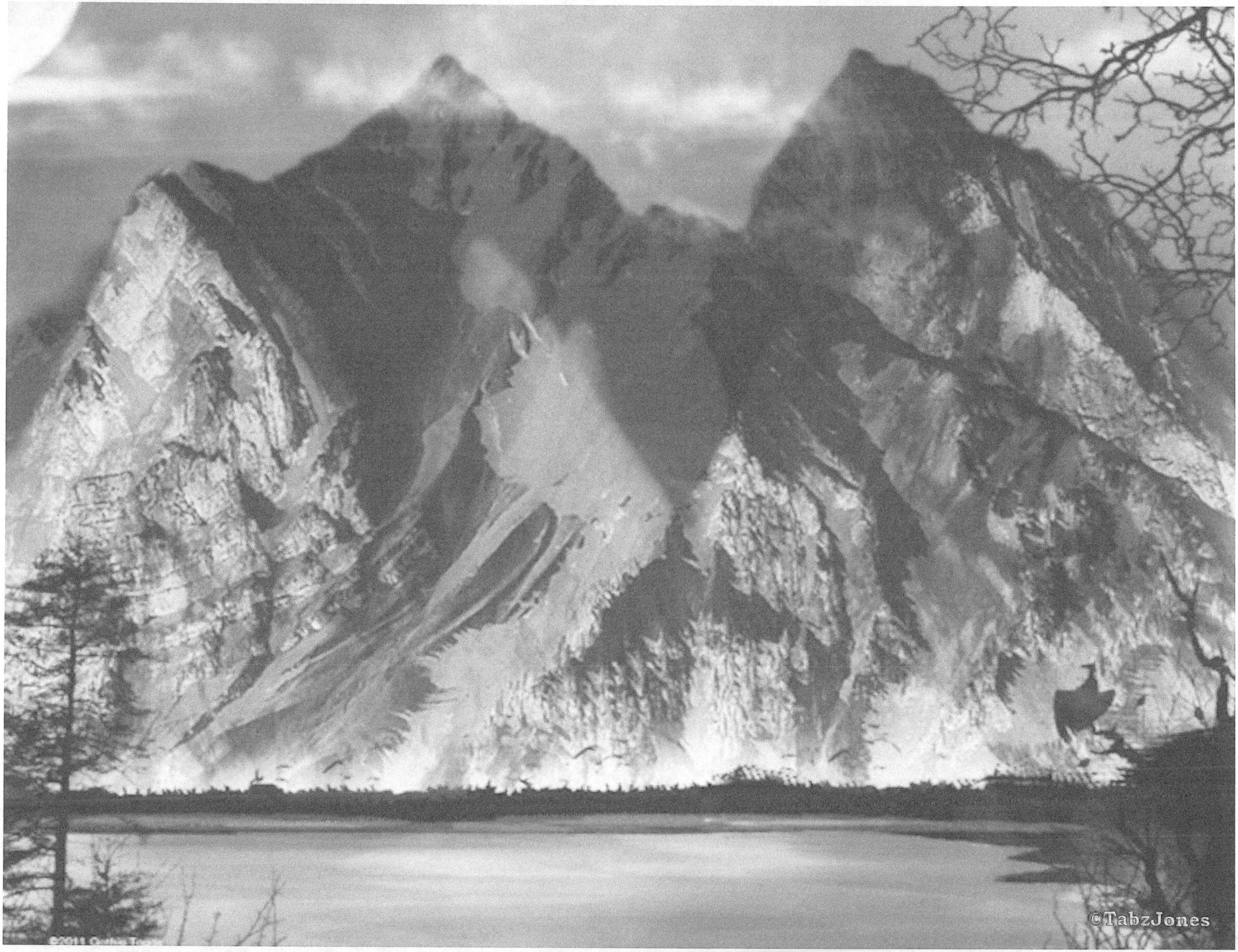
©TabzJones

www.ingramcontent.com/pod-product-compliance
Lightning Source LLC
Chambersburg PA
CBHW080606190526
45169CB00007B/2909